PENELOPE'S FOREVER PACIFIER

Deborah Morrow

Copyright © Deborah Morrow 2024 All rights reserved. No part of this book may be reproduced or used in any manner without written permission of the copyright owner except for the use of quotations in a book review. For more information visit: deborahmorrowauthor@gmail.com

ISBN: 978-1-0690120-3-6

Illustrated by Kath Grimshaw

Publisher's Note: This is a work of fiction. All of the characters, places, and situations portrayed in this book are the products of the author's imagination. Any correlations to real life are purely coincidental.

DEDICATION

For my granddaughter, Lilah who loves her 'passo' no matter what.

ACKNOWLEDGEMENTS

Thanks to Irene Cant
for her wisdom and support.

Penelope loved her pacifier and no matter what, she wouldn't give it up.
"I'm keeping it forever," said Penelope.

Everyone in the family tried different ways to get the pacifier away from Penelope, but nothing was working. They were all worried that Penelope was too old for a pacifier, except for Grandma that is.

"Give her time," said Grandma, "she will give up her pacifier when she's ready."

But the family did not want to give her time and they thought of clever ways to get Penelope to let her pacifier go.

Mommy offered to trade the pacifier for a new story book about glorious green galaxies in outer space.

Nanny offered to trade
a big fluffy brown teddy
bear to cuddle.

Big Brother offered to trade his favourite T-Rex that roared when its button was pushed.

Big Sister offered to trade her special red fire truck that had flashing lights and a real siren.

Uncle offered to trade a pink cupcake with swirly icing and sweet sugary sprinkles.

Cousin offered to trade her cosmic kaleidoscope, but Penelope wouldn't budge.

She just wasn't ready to give up her pacifier.

"She can't go to outer space with a pacifier," said Mommy.

"She can't be a police constable with a pacifier," said Nanny.

"She can't be a doctor with a pacifier," said Big Brother.

"She can't be a ballerina with a pacifier," said Big Sister.

"She can't teach science class with a pacifier," said Uncle.

"She can't be a movie star with a pacifier," said Cousin.

"Give her time," said Grandma, "she will give up her pacifier when she's ready."

But everyone else thought
that Penelope would
never be ready.

Springtime arrived at Penelope's house and the Easter Bunny came and went.

Summer sandcastles at Cobbly Beach Cottage came and went.

Hallowe'en trick or treating came and went and still Penelope showed no signs of giving up her pacifier.

Everyone was getting even more worried. They all thought Penelope would be the first person in the world to graduate from school with a pacifier in her mouth.

Grandma smiled and told them, "Penelope will give up her pacifier when she's ready and it won't be too long, I promise."

When Christmas came, Grandma began making decorations for the tree. On the table were little silver jingle bells, shimmery tinsel, sparkly gold stars, tiny shiny fairy lights, red, purple and blue glitter, brightly painted buttons and ribbons in every colour of the rainbow.

Grandma asked Penelope if she would like to make a new ornament for the Christmas tree. "I have an idea for an ornament," said Penelope.

"Are you sure?" Asked Grandma.

"Yes," said Penelope, "I'm sure."

Penelope spent hours decorating her ornament with silver bells, glitter, tinsel and brightly coloured buttons.

She wrapped it up with tiny shiny fairy lights and tied a green ribbon around it.

Grandma helped Penelope hang her new sparkling decoration on the twinkling Christmas tree.

And that is how Penelope kept her pacifier forever...

...Even in outer space.